Carnivals 2

THEME PARKS

School Leadership Strategies

that create a desired, attractive climate!

Jack Birmingham, Jr.

Prologue

After 24 years in education in 6 different school settings, I was blessed to be named the building principal of an elementary school that housed students from grades Kindergarten through 5th grade. While it was not my first administrative position, nor the first time to lead a group of people, it WAS my first opportunity to lead a building and create the climate that I felt would best serve my students. I had the confidence to be effective and knew that I could fall back on the various positions to help guide me. My thirteen years serving as an Athletic Director, Head Basketball coach and Assistant Principal indeed helped me prepare for what would lie ahead. However, as I sat in my office on a quiet July day in 2012, I needed to come to grips with what I want my building to become. I had yet to really meet with our students, staff and parents so the canvas I needed to paint was blank. I began to think about the things that I particularly enjoyed when I attended school and even more so, what aspects of my own four children's education helped each of them succeed? As a teacher, what type of leadership did I appreciate the most and how did that style help me become a confident, successful teacher?

As I began to consider these factors, I realized that I now had an incredible responsibility to our school community to create a climate that everyone would enjoy. THIS would be the best way for our students to succeed. At the end of the day, that is all that matters.

Throughout my first year I began to work with my students, staff and parents to develop solid relationships. In this process, I could see that developing trust, respect and fun lead to wonderful opportunities to build a great climate. As my years progressed and our climate strengthened, I felt moved to put these strategies to pen and share them. While this book will discuss strategies for building leaders, I have encouraged teachers to use these in their classroom as well.

Carnivals 2 Theme Parks was born out of my educational experiences and my love for amusement parks. A simple comparison that we can all relate to, as educators look for ways to make their buildings and classrooms warm and welcoming places to help student academic and social growth.

On a personal note, the successes that I have experienced along my career would not be possible without the encouragement of my wonderful wife Doreen. She has been a wonderful support for me and a Godly mother to our four children, Tyler, Maranda, Gracie and Serena. For that I am eternally grateful.

Introduction

During the 1970s, as the summer days rolled on, there was a special feeling of fun and excitement which came as an annual rite of passage to a kid in Northeast Ohio. Long before smart phones, Netflix and even Atari, I was the typical kid who had to be doing something outdoors, such as, frequenting our city swimming pool or playing third base in little league. Growing up in a steel worker's family, I found great enjoyment in the little things and anytime there was a trip to the local church festival or county fair on the family agenda, I was ready and willing! There was nothing better than getting the glow in the dark wristbands or hand stamps to 'ride all day' on the Tilt-a-Whirl, Ferris Wheel or Dodge 'em Cars! I am not sure that I would be able to tell you today what caused such excitement as a kid, except for the fact that these places contained thrills, chills and smiles!

Now while these "day trips" were some of my most precious memories during my adolescent summers, they paled in comparison to when we first experienced "the land of the mouse" affectionately known as Walt Disney World. Now THIS was the trip!

It was the trip that we all looked forward to. Well, maybe getting there was not the best of experiences, as a 22- hour road trip in a Ford Country Squire wasn't exactly arriving in first class. I have some details about that for later in the book. Disney World and many other theme parks across our land have become desired destinations for thousands of families. They are unlike the carnivals that come parading into your town and, within a few days, construct a glitzy world of fun, highlighted by snazzy rides with clever names. These thrill-seeking attractions temporarily cover up the pavement where basketball and foursquare was played during recess of a church school or the saw dust of a county fair's grandstand track.

The "theme" parks as they are known have become the places that fathers and mothers set aside money to give their children a once in a lifetime experience. They are the places that my mom and dad would bring the 8mm video camera to and record every memory that was made. Then, five months later, fire up the projector, set up a K-mart bought screen and show these bizarre, colored, silent movies of my family strolling the grounds of the Magic Kingdom to our entire extended family during a holiday visit.

Throughout my career in education, I have come to the realization that as building leaders, our schools should be a place that our families and students look forward to being a part of! We must work to get our schools to create a climate that parents make a point to attend and tell their families about the experiences when they get together at Christmas time, without the 8mm family movies, of course. I believe leaders must strive to make their school one that resembles these theme parks that stand the test of time and have wonderful appeal, as opposed to the temporary festivals that have short-lived glitz and glamour that only entice visitors because of its sudden appearance on the landscape.

Throughout this book, I will take you on a journey that will hopefully recall some wonderful memories from your childhood and intertwine them with how we can create a climate, that over time, will morph into a culture that is conducive to a sustained wonderful learning environment. Additionally, I will share some strategies that have proven successful to address three important areas of climate development and workspaces for you to jot down your strategies that you would like to try.

As you begin to reflect on your school ask yourself, how is your climate? Is it something that can positively grow into a sustained cultural change in three to five years? Ask yourself three simple questions.

1. Do you believe that your students want to come to your building?
2. Do you feel that your staff members enjoy coming to work?
3. Do you believe that your families (parents) feel comfortable in your school?

If you are not sure about any of these questions, this book will help you develop a plan to strengthen these relationships.

We will discover how **trust**, **respect** and **fun** are the fundamental ideals that building leaders can use to create a great climate. You might just get some cotton candy on your fingers as we progress...but that is perfectly fine!

Construction Factors

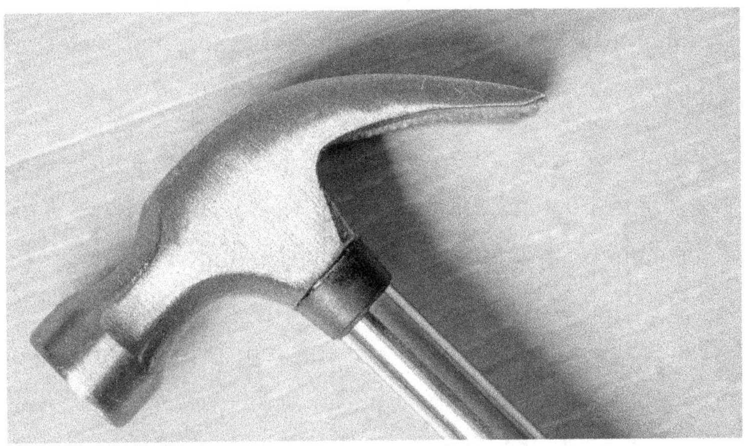

What you need to know and focus on before you begin to build your climate.

As you begin to plan your great transformation of moving your building from a simple carnival climate to that of a theme park, we need to identify the THREE most important groups of people that you must develop relationships with as you lead a building. With each group you will have an opportunity to develop a sense of trust, respect and fun to help nurture your building's environment.

The first group and the most important is that of your STUDENTS. We are in this business for kids. So, as you begin to evaluate your current and/or future climate, remember to focus on the things that matter most. A building leader, who can create strong relationships with their students, is on the fast track to an effective place of learning.

Secondly, we will look at your STAFF as an influential group in climate building. In fact, they may be one of the most challenging of the groups, which will require more work on your part. At times, outside factors in their own personal lives get in the way of the development and this may slow your process. Throughout the book I will share ways to address your staff and encourage them to be vital factors in your new theme park.

The last group of importance in setting the tone for your climate is your stakeholders. These are primarily your parents and guardians who have vested interests in your school. This group differs from grades Kindergarten through twelfth grade as their views of school change. The elementary stakeholders have a different view of climate than that of middle or high school stakeholders. The strategies and ideas that will be shared can work at any grade level and any school.

One group that is not specifically mentioned in these THREE would be Central office and Board members. While every building leader realizes the importance that this group of individuals' have, it must be understood that when a principal creates a climate of trust, respect and fun with the three aforementioned groups, this fourth group will be equally pleased with the effects of the "new theme park" in their district.

As you begin to review how to approach this building process, keep in mind that in order to achieve the true "theme park" level of building climate, eventually the trust, respect and fun factors need to be mutually developed within the three groups. In other words, it will be the final goal to have mutual respect with Students, and mutual trust with Staff, etc. (see fig.1).

When you strengthen these factors within each of your main groups, there will be an equal flow returning to your office. In a successful theme park, the employees gain as much enjoyment by simply watching the patrons enjoy themselves. Seems strange but it most certainly occurs. This is eventually the climate you would desire to build in your school.

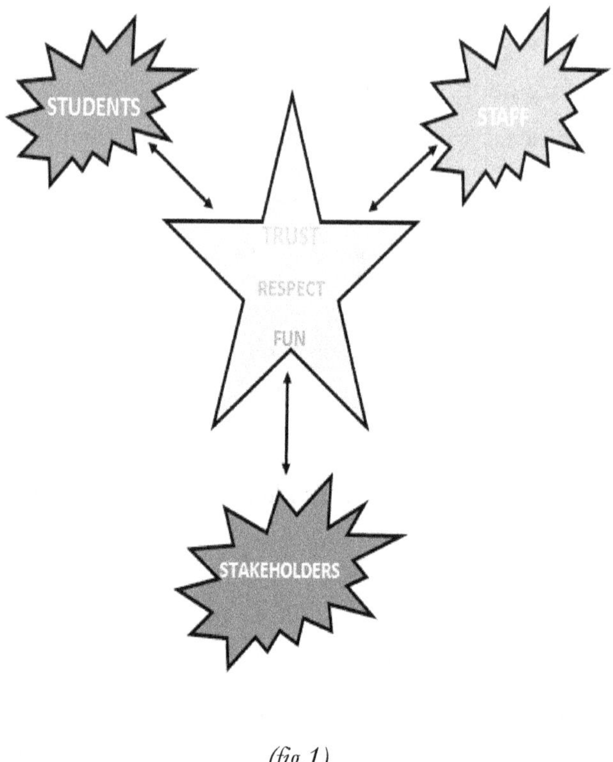

(fig.1)

In the following chapters, we will explore the specifics to address each group by focusing on these factors. It is important to understand that <u>YOU MUST</u> develop all three factors of trust, respect and fun to build a successful climate for your transformation. Think of it as a three-legged stool. Each leg needs the other two to stay upright. A simple but true visual when understanding their importance in the foundation of your theme park.

Trust

Developing **<u>TRUST</u>** with your students, staff and stakeholders.

Students (TRUST)

Do the students that you are entrusted to, TRUST you? So how does the trust of a patron affect the climate of a successful theme park? Well, imagine you were in line for one of the world's highest, longest, fastest coasters (which on a side note I believe exists at EVERY theme park for some reason). You had just passed the sign that reads "From HERE it is a 60-minute wait" and you can now begin to see the monstrous coaster you have signed up for and more importantly, the workers in the station who are going to assist you. You see how they give every rider step by step instructions for THEIR safety and they even double check one's ability to buckle themselves. They TELL you that your safety is their priority and you realize this truth by what you see.

Now, try going on a ride of that magnitude with no directions or safety checks and my guess would be you would not need a sign that says "From HERE it is a 60 minute wait" but rather a sign that say - "Before you enter our ride, we just want to wish you good luck….hope to see you when you exit!"

As we begin to look at how we best develop the climate for our building, THE most important group to focus on is our students. They are the life of the school. Every day when they arrive, we don't know what they are bringing with them physically, emotionally, economically or socially. Much like the great theme parks these students should be welcomed with a smile and a "glad you are here" each and EVERY day. The time they spend at your school may be the BEST part of their day and the reality of their life reappears once they return home. This is the glamour and excitement of our theme parks as well. For a time, we can escape the cruel realities of the world and enjoy life!

As we look to develop trust with our students the simplest way to do that is simply show the students that you've "got their back…….in everything!" From school safety, to their successes let them know that you care about them. If a student can walk into your school and feel like he trusts you running the school, that is one less thing they need to worry about, and they can focus on other things to enhance their experience. So how does a building leader go about showing trust? I have always felt that the best way a building leader can promote trust is by being visible. For instance, if you tell your students that you are going to support them in their different activities, such as concerts, contests and school plays, make sure that you attend them and make a point to speak with them, so they know YOU WERE THERE! This is tremendously important.

When a student asks you during the school day, "Mr. B did you see my game last night?" If you went to the game, make sure to be able to recall something from that experience. A simple "yes I did...and those two free throws you hit in the third quarter were clutch" response will go miles in building trust with that student! They want to see that you truly DO care about them in every aspect of their education. Your presence will send a wonderful message to back up your support.

Additionally, in my building I would often tell my students that their safety is my top priority. To build the trust with them, they would often times see me doing "walk arounds" at my school. A simple lap on the exterior of my building to ensure that the school is secure and that there are no safety concerns was a routine that I had established within my W.E.L.C.O.M.E. Mat strategy that I will share later in the book. Not only is it valuable for the aforementioned safety measures, but I often would get students waving to me as I walk around. They know that Mr. Birmingham is looking out for them…that is priceless in developing their trust.

Our theme parks want you to trust them with you and your family's security and safety as well. You can't walk too far in any major theme park and NOT see a sign about safety. From specific ride safety, to protocol for lost children, guests can see that their own well-being is first and foremost in the minds of the theme parks. Safety, security and comfort is established in advance and carefully planned out for an enjoyable experience. One exception might be the "plan" to place the "All-American" concession building, home of the Megatron Nacho and Chili Cheese Mountain o' Fries, immediately adjacent to the Scrambler ride. Those don't mix well…ever. Just sayin'.

Suggestions to build TRUST with your STUDENTS

❏ Pick a few Little League games to attend.

❏ Share with your students what you and the teachers do for their safety at school.

❏ Select random students' pieces of work and have them share their thoughts with you on how they develop them. Make a point to tell them how much you appreciate their efforts in doing their very best.

❏ Attend as many concerts and plays that you can and more importantly, talk with those students who were involved, the next day at school.

Staff (TRUST)

Do your staff members trust you as their leader? Much like the students in the building, a school's staff needs to know that they can trust the person who is leading them. Trust in not only how they lead a building for the academic growth of the students, but in all areas. Staff members need to know that their leader trusts them in the classroom and every aspect of serving. You can tell your staff that you trust them, but your actions will speak louder than your words. Teachers can be very fragile in their profession. The trust-building is a gradual process that will not happen overnight, however, it is instrumental for the school's climate. If your staff do not trust you, they will stay guarded and will not feel comfortable enough to step out of their comfort zone to stretch themselves to grow.

So how do you go about building up trust with your staff? Start by sticking to your word! When you have discussions with your staff be careful of the promises that you make. I am not saying to avoid promises, but rather, know that EVERY promise that you make must be followed through. If for some reason you cannot make good on a promise, at least let them know why. For instance, I want my teachers to step out of their comfort zone during classroom observations and try new things. Instead of simply presenting a lesson to their students, I want to get a sense of how they teach on an average day. I then reinforce to them that I am not worrying about "little things" that you can't control as you teach. I want to see the flow of a classroom when minor disruptions occur, such as office announcements, student interruptions or even off topic bandits. This occurs every day in their classroom and I want them to feel confident to move from the "stand and deliver" approach to a more typical lesson that may include stations, technology or other methods.

Now, WHAT I CAN'T DO, is evaluate them poorly in an area that they may have been successful if they were doing the stand and deliver approach. This will be detrimental to what I am trying to accomplish. In contrast, their evaluations are laced with praise for them stepping "outside of their comfort zone" to try new things. Happy employees are vital to the positive environment of the workplace. Finding a disgruntled Disney employee would be like finding a unicorn.

Additionally, your staff will need to know that you show support for them if a conflict arises between a teacher and a parent. While I may not always agree with the teacher in a particular issue and even see merit on the parent's side, ONE thing that they know is that I ALWAYS side on what's best for the child. Thus, I am not favoring one over the other, but like them, I focus on the growth of a student. If teachers feel that you will ALWAYS side with a parent in a disagreement, there will be a constant desire to avoid any potential conflict with their students' parents and thus not remove all barriers for the betterment of their class.

You can also build their trust by helping them when there is a need. I have always maintained an open-door policy in my office. My staff knew that they never need an appointment and can come to me about anything. This closeness helps build and unite your family. They know that if at any time there is a personal issue that they need to address immediately, I will support them in anyway. Although, be VERY careful about declaring this statement to your staff. I found out one week into my first year as a Principal that a kindergarten class can be vicious!!!

After declaring to my staff that if they ever have a family emergency and need to leave, we will always have their back. In fact, I declared, 'that even if we can't get your class covered, I would step in to allow them to address the family need".

Of course, as luck would have it, our Kindergarten class needed immediate coverage and this principal came to the rescue! Then ten minutes later I needed rescued! Kindergarten to me was like herding cats, who ask questions about…anything. But in the end, I kept my word to that teacher, created a few laughs with the staff and began to build the all-important trust.

<u>**Suggestions to build TRUST with your STAFF**</u>

- ❏ If a teacher has a family issue and needs to arrive or leave early, allow them the flexibility. In fact, if you are able, cover the class for them!

- ❏ At a staff meeting lead a conversation on "trust". Ask for ideas on how trust is earned and/or lost.

- ❏ Have an open-door policy with all of your teachers and let them "vent" to you at times.

- ❏ If you messed up, apologize! Show your human side.

- ❏ Delegate important responsibilities to your staff members and follow up with words of encouragement for what they accomplished. Be sure to align the job with the competency level of the staff member, so that success is a strong probability.

Parents (TRUST)

The third important factor in creating a climate of trust is the connection you have between you and the stakeholders/parents of your school. Let's face it. They are sending you their most precious commodities and need to have the confidence that their children will be safe and challenged educationally. Do the parents trust you with their child? This trust is unique in the fact, that some of it is formed through their own eyes, while other parts are strengthened through word of mouth.

At times, students are the conduit of information to the home for the events of the day at school. While I would send home many communiques about what occurs at school, the students still would share things from their own viewpoint. I stressed to the parents that we were going to challenge students academically while keeping them physically and socially safe. Additionally, I wanted the students to be able to share with their parents pieces of evidence that we are working hard at our objective.

If I tell the stakeholders that school safety in our school is a high priority, I want them to physically SEE me making steps to keeping their children safe, much like those rollercoaster operators! I had created a method to remind myself to do this, for which I will share in the coming pages, but if parents can view first hand your methods for keeping a safe environment, they will feel comfortable about sending their children to your school...and yes they will talk to other parents about it as well!

For instance, on our opening day of school in my first year as building principal, I was informed that we had a strange vehicle in the parking lot adjacent to our playground during recess. It appeared from the eyes of our supervisors that a person was sitting in the car watching the students play. Upon hearing this I walked out and unintentionally startled a mother who had wanted to simply watch her new kindergartner at recess on his first day! While there was no safety concern after she identified herself, the comments around the neighborhood about "the principal who quickly came out to investigate a strange vehicle" were valuable to begin establishing trust!!

<u>**Suggestions to gain TRUST with Parents.**</u>

❑ Be visible in your school, particularly before and after school.

❑ Take new parents on a tour of your school. Don't let office staff do this. You can use this time to share your heart with new families.

❑ Tell parents how school safety is very important to you. (See W.E.L.C.O.M.E. Mat on next page.)

❑ Be quick to communicate with your school parents about concerns, changes or specific events. They will appreciate that you are on top of these things that are important to them.

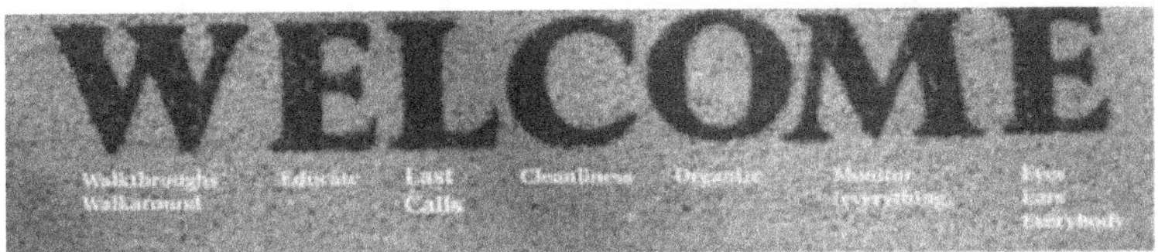

The W.E.L.C.O.M.E. Mat

We want our school to be a welcoming place that families' desire to be, much like your own home. Many homes display their public welcome by laying a "Welcome Mat" at the base of the front door. Using the word "welcome" I have created a quick reminder to help me stay on top of things that may hurt the trust I am trying to build for my students, staff and stakeholders.

The **W** stands for walk arounds or walk-throughs within your own building to ensure its security and to be aware of anything that might affect it. I try and do a simple walk around of the outside of my building at least once a week and walk through classrooms daily to keep my eyes open for things that may seem strange or pose any hidden dangers. It's an easy habit to get into! While seeing areas that need touched up or some safety hazards that need to be addressed are first and foremost, the simple appearance of me walking around or through my building speaks volumes to the students, staff and even parents who see me take my "walk"! It also serves as a great therapeutic escape from the mundane duties of my office and gives me great joy to just simply walk through a classroom with a smile and check on the students or let a teacher know that I appreciate what they are doing! Simultaneously I am looking at doors, windows, desks, corners, edges, lights, and anything else that could be a hidden hazard to those in the classroom. So yes, basically I become my father, who, when he became a grandpa, displayed the incredible quickness and skill of walking in front of or behind each of his grandchildren and looked out for things that may hurt them. I don't believe any of my children ever walked by an end table or coffee table without grandpa's hand covering the corner! Ironically, I had numerous stitches from hitting my head on a window seal or running into a bed corner…funny how that works.

The **E** stands for the "education" of my staff, students and community about school safety. I continue to teach them about school safety and ways that we all can keep our school a safe place. This builds trust with them by simply reviewing different strategies and making the time to focus on safety drills such as fire, tornado and lock downs. Additionally, I work with them on even the day-to-day procedures to help our environment. Unfortunately, society has shown all of us that the days of assuming the safety of our schools is a thing of the past, so we need to constantly build up our defenses against the evils of this world. By educating the precious souls in my school, I exhibit a love for them that fortifies their trust in me.

The **L** of W.E.L.C.O.M.E stands for "last calls" and these are my favorite!   When you want a tool that will build trust for your students, staff and even your parents I <u>highly recommend using these</u>! Last calls are simply phone calls that I make at the end of the day that started as a way of me ending my day on a positive note. We all know as building leaders that there are many times when we have to make phone calls which we are not crazy about, simply because of the potential confrontation of upset parents. We sometimes take that home with us and I came to the realization that I wanted to end every day on a positive note. With that in mind, I requested from my staff members to give me names of students who may have done a great thing throughout the school day and I make a list to call those parents as my "last calls" of the day. These phone calls take literally one minute to make. Sometimes the parent answers and sometimes I get their voicemail. Either way works for me! In fact, voicemail messages can be even more productive as I have had parents tell me that they save the message from me and they replay it at times.

These calls always end positively, and the most important factor of this phone call is ending with a complement to the parents for doing a great job on raising their child! It goes without saying how incredible these calls are in developing trust with my parents and stakeholders. I have had compliments from parents about the "last calls" and in fact, in a school neighborhood the word quickly gets out when a parent receives a phone call like this. They don't shy away from talking about their principal who took time to tell them how great their child is! Who needs those "my son made the honor roll sticker" on the back of the minivan?

Equally, last calls are great to use on my own staff. I have had staff members drop me a note to do a last call for a teacher who may have spent some extra time helping them with a lesson or brought in a delicious lunch treat. When I get these, I make a point to leave a voice message so that they have a special treat when they arrive home. As a teacher, hearing this message from the principal is nice, however, knowing that one of your fellow staff members nominated you to receive it, is worth its weight in gold! Much like finishing the coolest roller coaster ride of your life, sitting in the front car, and having the hard hat wearing ride operator announce, have another ride on us. Life is good at that theme park!

C stands for cleanliness. As the building leader I try to focus on keeping our school clean in as many ways as possible. I meet regularly with our custodial staff to discuss areas that need to be addressed and also find ways to help them out as well. My philosophy is by keeping our school clean, we create a sense of pride and more importantly, people will WANT to come to our school. Again, I want a theme park atmosphere! Every theme park takes pride in their clean appearance. From the shiny rides and clean restrooms to those employees walking the midway with the brooms and "dustpans on a stick" hunting stray snow cone wrappers and cotton candy sticks, you can't help but notice the overall effort of making your experience a memorable one. The cleanliness of our school says much about our school pride and it encourages and shows parents that we care about the building that they are sending their children to.

The **O** stands for the organization of drills, plans and other important documents that I can easily get to. My "welcome mat" has a primary focus on school safety to help fortify the trust of the students, staff and stakeholders. It is important that I show them I am knowledgeable when it comes to their safety. Being organized with my fire and tornado drills as well as school lockdowns will create a sense of comfort that adds to the trust I am trying to build. As you work on your organization, don't skip over the small stuff. Be educated on every aspect of your building and keep good records of when you drilled and any issues that occurred. Additionally, work closely with fire, police and maintenance personnel when conducting drills. Their professional insight is priceless. From evacuation positions to heating and air-conditioning systems, the advice you can gain from them will help keep you organized and show your school that there is a united team working for their safety.

The **M** reminds me to monitor my surroundings. Be in tune with not just inclement weather, but also take note of strange cars, odd noises, unique smells, etc. Develop that sixth sense as a school leader so you are aware of different things as you walk your hallways. As I continue to do this, I encourage my staff members to do the same. A recess aide's "sixth sense" lead to the aforementioned report of a stranger in a strange car at a recess.

And lastly the **E** within our welcome mat stands for eyes and ears. These are very important to have your students and staff focus on everything they see and hear. First reporting is crucial to teach them the importance of sharing strange things that occur even if it's the most mundane concept. It's not wrong to simply say that there is somebody outside or something is not right. I educate them that we can always check that later.

This welcome mat is a great tool to simply follow. Have it posted in your office and take a look at that every morning to see which of these letters you need to hit that day. This will go a long way in building the trust that you so desperately want to build in your development to create a great theme park of our school.

When It Rains at the Park!

So, you have planned out your entire trip and completed your yearlong calendar countdown to the family trip of a lifetime. You have purchased your matching family Hawaiian shirts (I hear people do this...don't judge me) and when you arrive on Day one as you walk into the park the heavens open and a torrential downpour occurs! When planning vacations, you prepare for unexpected weather and equally we must prepare for unexpected speed bumps as we try to strengthen these three components in our building.

Your leadership and decisions will be scrutinized at times and the trust you are hoping for may not have worked out the way you were hoping. You may feel that your staff members are still apprehensive about your efforts to trust them. Don't quit. When you feel that you have demonstrated trust to your staff members, DEMONSTRATE MORE! When you feel that your stakeholders don't trust you leading their building, DO MORE! When you think that your students don't trust you in keeping them safe SHOW MORE!

Building trust at times is not easy. It doesn't always work out the way you hope. You may need to do some research on those people who need to trust you and find out what they look for. Ask them! Remember that YOU can control this development. If you were planning to head out to the theme park and saw rain in the forecast, you would start to research alternative activities. Sometimes trust can get even stronger through perseverance.

After gathering so much information over the years pertaining to School Safety, it can be overwhelming as a building leader. Thus I created a quick reminder for myself and then aligned it to what I want my building to be. A place for everyone to feel "Welcome."

W- Walk-arounds and/or walk-throughs within your building.

E- Educate.....your staff, students and community about school safety.

L- "last calls" that I make to homes of students who have had a good day. This helps promote self-esteem for our students.

C- Cleanliness....keep your building clean which helps create a sense of pride!

O- organization of drills, plans and other important documents that you can easily get to.

M- Monitor...ALWAYS monitor your surroundings. Strange cars, inclement weather, noises, etc.

E –eyes and ears...these are very important to have your students and staff!! Teach them to use them ALWAYS and report strange things...

Respect

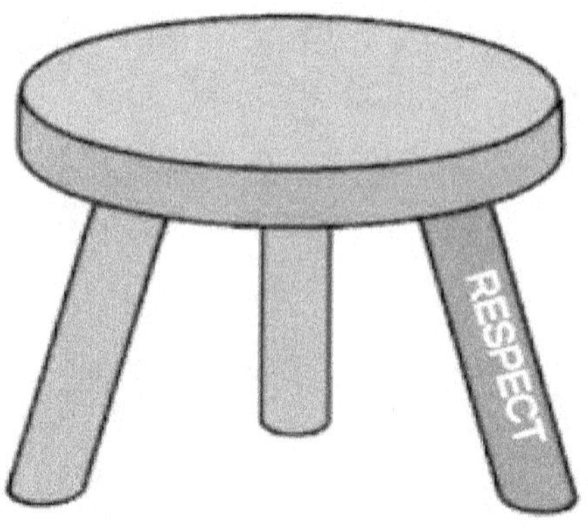

Looking for ways to build a mutual RESPECT with your students, staff and stakeholders.

A second important leg of the school climate stool is that of respect. As building leader, you must learn to respect those you are working with, those you are educating and those who send their precious cargo to you. When each of our three groups realize that you truly respect them for who they are and what they have done, the climate will strengthen both internally and externally. As we think about our school trying to emulate a wonderfully desirable theme park, imagine, if you will, a destination that DOESN'T respect you, your family and your finances!

Major theme parks try very hard to be respectful and grateful for the time and money we spend to visit them. That is why you see and hear words like "thank you", "how can we help" and "we will miss you" throughout these parks. They respect us from the moment we step into the park and greet us with a smile. Did I mention that a smile is a MAJOR part of respect??

There is something special when those "way too happy" employees of any theme park are waiting in their brightly colored outfits to sing you a happy song of welcoming that truly only has the words "happy", "welcome" and "lalala" in it. But you know what? It works! It doesn't matter how far we drove, how hot the car was, how cramped the back seat was, or how much your moms and dads shelled out for this trip!

The employees and administration of the park get it. They know what it takes to sacrifice to come to "their" park and they work very hard for you to feel respected! When we are leading a building, we need to make sure that our students, staff and stakeholders have that same feeling when they arrive. You might not need to wear the brightly colored outfits and sing the corny welcoming song, but you know what? Sometimes they work!! Let's take a look at how we can specifically show respect to strengthen our climate.

Students (RESPECT)

One of the most difficult things for educators to do would be to respect each and every student that they come into contact with. For when we deal with so many student behaviors, backgrounds and challenges, it is very easy to take it personally when we are "disrespected" and then we want to give it back! Students, no matter the age, want to be respected. They seek this from their families and friends and, believe it or not, they want to be respected by their teachers and administrators. If you can think about how many times students had no desire to come to school, in all of those times, how would that change if they knew at least ONE school staff member respected them for who they are? If a school's student population feels respected by the adults in the building, it will then seep into the peer relations and respect, in general, will increase and you will be able to see a noticeable change in your climate!

One way that you can immediately begin respecting your students is to KNOW THEIR NAMES! It seems silly, but if you don't take time to remember their names, how much will they feel you respect them as a person? How have you felt when someone forgot your name, or didn't take the time to know exactly how to pronounce it? Take it from a kid whose last name is Birmingham (Bingham, Binghamton, Burningham, the list goes on!).

When you make the time to really get to know something about a student you show them the respect that they so desire. Make connections and not just the generic connection. Show interest in the things your kids like. If you have a student who is struggling academically because he loves playing video games, FIND OUT WHAT GAMES HE LIKES AND LEARN ABOUT THAT GAME! Learn enough to have conversations with him. This shows him that you respect and care about him. The academics will come with time but develop a respectful connection first!

- ❑ Make a point to memorize as many students as possible in your building. Start by Grade level with a roster of students.

- ❑ Establish meetings with student council, clubs and teams to allow them a chance to have a voice in their education.

- ❑ Develop a principal's advisory group to talk about weekly happenings.

- ❑ Create a Happy Birthday plan where you send birthday wishes to each student.

- ❑ Make a Good News bulletin board and simply put a student's name on the board. No real reason needs to be stated. Just that the Good News shows your students "making a difference"! This allows for ALL students to have a chance to be put on the Good News bulletin board.

<u>Staff</u> (RESPECT)

I believe that this is THE MOST IMPORTANT aspect of our climate that must be maintained and strengthened constantly if your school is ever going to move from a carnival to a theme park. Teachers, not unlike students, need the reassurance that their building leader respects what they do and the challenges of their job. Make sure that you show respect to your staff members, and yes, at times, certain staff members can make it very difficult to respect them. Their negative attitudes and condescending eye rolls make it a challenge but respecting them takes away their excuses to be that way!

I have always made a point to refer to each staff member as a professional. Society tends to forget that teachers and administrators spend many hours and hard- earned dollars to get where they are. I make a point to tell the teachers to "be proud of their accomplishments"! Encourage them to display their diplomas, accomplishments and teacher licenses in their classrooms. This sends a great message to students and parents when they enter their room. Remember, that you want to move your school from a carnival, which typically employs volunteers to take tickets, dish out elephant ears and the 48-hour trained "Carnies"! Our theme park needs to have respected employees.

Along with the respect of their education, don't forget to respect their life! What I mean by that is, appreciate how their life can get in the way of school. We all have times in our lives that encompass our everyday activities and make it very difficult for us to function. Tell the teachers that you understand that and, more importantly, make a point to find out about how things are going for them.

One strategy that we implemented each and every year was to have the staff members share what their favorite snack, candy and drink was. My office would keep these forms on file and use them if there was ever a time that I felt one of them could use a pick me up. For example, when one of my teachers had just sent their last child off to college the weekend before this particular Monday morning, I went to our "pick-me-up" file and made a quick trip to our nearby gas station/convenient store to grab the teacher's favorites. When I returned to school, I bee-lined it to her room, walked in unannounced, and set them on her desk. My only words to her were simply, "just because"! This doesn't take much, however, the results and impact of doing something like this is worth its weight in gold. Now here is the disclaimer. The GOOD news is that your teacher will tell the rest of the staff how thoughtful and respectful you were as a building leader for doing that. The BAD news is that your teacher will tell the rest of the staff how thoughtful and respectful you were! So... you are going to have to do that a lot! And that is exactly how you create a building of respect for your staff members.

When these things happen, staff members will WANT to come and be a part of this theme park!

One final point of building the respect was discovered with the gas station/convenient store owner who noticed my visits and the period to purchases of various candy bars, chips and soft drinks. On some repeat visits, his comment was not "Jack you may want to try some healthier options," but rather, "so another teacher needing a pick-me-up, huh?"

Yet another path to spreading the word in your community about this theme park you are building!

❏ Have your staff participate in the "Compliment Carousel. This is a wonderful activity that can be done any time of the school year. It may be a good idea to do this around the Holidays! Simply make copies of your teaching staff and/or complete staff, depending on the size. (Larger schools may need to break these down by grade level or even departments) Have your teachers write ONE positive sentence about each teacher on the list and then collect them. Take some time to review the compliments and pick three or four of the compliments on a separate card for each teacher. They will now each have a card of four compliments that their colleagues said about them! Priceless.

❏ Create the "Snack Pick-Me-Up" list. At the beginning of the school year have your staff fill out their favorite drink (that can be consumed legally in schools!), favorite candy and favorite snack. Collect these and keep them in a handy place. Then look for opportunities to use these to help pick up a staff member who may be having a tough day.

<u>Parents</u> (RESPECT)

As the building leader, if you want the parents and stakeholders to respect you and your efforts for taking on this monumental task of running a building, you must make certain that you return the respect back to them. It is not very easy to be a parent. Period! Believe it or not the parents of your school are doing the very best they can. In some cases, they are parenting the way their parents raised them. I have often felt that when I share with the parents that I understand the struggles for which they face raising children it creates a nice simple bond to build on with them. This allows them to open up with me about any number of topics, from their child's education to why the US Flag hasn't been replaced! Remember as you move toward creating a "theme park" climate, think of how the major amusement parks, in our country, show respect to those who pay for their time there. Surveys, help stations and other support systems often go unnoticed, yet demonstrate the respect the park has for their visitors. They respect the amount of time, money and unforeseen challenges that go with bringing a family on a long, event-filled, "Wally World" voyage.

In order to demonstrate respect to your parents and stakeholders, you must first be able to develop a sincere method of communication. We can stand at the front of the auditorium on back to school night and say "I respect what you do as a parent," however, if that is the last time a parent feels that from you it will be forgotten as quick as a ten dollar bill disappears buying a corn dog and a bag of chips in the concession stand. You need to be authentic!

One of the easiest and best ways that I would develop respect was utilizing the "last calls" that I had elaborated on within the W.E.L.C.O.M.E. Mat. Again, these were invaluable in showing parents respect. Additionally, I would communicate to parents monthly in my newsletter, parenting tips and tricks, from handling homework demands to unique ways to engage in a conversation with their student after school.

<u>Suggestions to **RESPECT your PARENTS**</u>

❏ Create a plan to make "last calls" to the families of students who did something special.

❏ Once a month, share a parenting tip for families in your newsletter.

❏ Set up monthly coffee talks with parents. This does not need to be as intimidating as it seems. You can simply randomly send an invitation to different parents each month. You won't be able to hit them all, however, just the concept of you welcoming them in can be very effective.

When You Lost the Fast Pass!

We all know that what we sometimes expect to happen doesn't always turn out how we planned it. For instance, if you buy a "fast pass" to ride the world's tallest, fastest, scariest, expensive merry-go-round and you STILL have to wait 15 minutes, that doesn't seem to be a "fast pass". Seems more like a slightly quicker slow line! Anyhow, you know what I mean.

There are many times when it is hard to respect teachers, students and parents. But YOU are the leader of ALL of them! I have always been someone who seeks to have joy in my family, friends and workplace. Most people are like that and if you are a leader who wants to move their carnival to a theme park you MUST find joy in what you do. Yes, again, it's hard, but it is like getting ready to participate in a water balloon fight with some friends on a hot summer day. We all want to get cooled off by the cold water in the balloons, and the best way to be "ambushed" by water balloons is to throw the first one…and five more will be coming back at you! Thus, why I challenge teachers and administrators by asking them "did you throw any water balloons this week?" If you want the joy or respect, be willing to throw the first one!

Fun!

Sharing the FUN with your students, staff and stakeholders!!

Let's face it, we ALL want to have fun. Not just girls, Miss Lauper. As we look at the final pillar in our climate development, this one is the easiest to talk about and is really the icing on the cake. If we truly want our school environment to transform into a theme park, fun HAS to be a component. What theme parks have you gone to where you left saying, "Yep, pretty boring. I would have rather scraped paint off of an old barn." Answer? None of them! In fact, truth be told, the fun is what truly brings us back. What specifically brings you back? It simply depends on your taste. Those you lead will have different tastes and concepts of what fun is, but you have to do your homework and find these things out. YOUR idea of fun and THEIR idea of fun may be on opposite ends of the spectrum, but you must find a way to make them "want to come back" to your school. Look, we all can't agree on what is fun for each of us at a theme park. Some love the thrill of roller coasters, some can't wait to see the musicals, and others love anything that takes you 300 feet in the air and simply drops you! It always has amazed me to see what excites folks at these parks. There are some rides, as I look back, that still amaze me.

How is it, for instance that we can wait 15 minutes in line to get on the "Dodge 'em Cars, sprint to our favorite colored car on a grease-slicked floor only to get in and try NOT to dodge any cars? On a personal note, for some reason I always found that car buried in the corner of six other cars, only to hear the operator say "turn the wheel to the right" for the first minute before I would be able to straighten my car! You know the worst thing that can happen to you is when the ride operator had to come out of his "command center", stand on the back of your car and straighten it out for you! In that case, when you exit the ride, head immediately to "kiddieland", or the bench on the merry-go-round for your next level of thrills. (Speaking of the "bench", who stands in line waiting for the merry-go-round and says to their friends, I don't want a horse I got the gold, diamond bench...I call?) But you know what? The theme parks KNOW that the bench IS fun to someone…they have done their homework!

<u>Students</u> (FUN)

Your students want to enjoy themselves at school. Yes, I know that most students can't wait for weekends, holidays and summer vacation, but if they HAVE to be there, they would prefer to have fun! As you lead a building having fun with your students may take on different forms depending on their age. Additionally, you will see that the trust and respect that you have developed with them will allow for more opportunities to do some crazy things. Don't be afraid to make yourself vulnerable to give your student body an opportunity to see you as a "human" and not just the robotic building leader that they see every day. Take chances! In my years of leading a building I have had the wonderful opportunity to kiss a pig, get smacked in the face with a pie, play the part of Santa's elf at our family Christmas night, be duct taped to a wall, dress up like former Chicago Bears coach Mike Ditka dancing along to the Super Bowl shuffle (true sacrifice from a diehard Cleveland Browns fan) and even play the guitar during a spring outdoor music gala. These are just a few of the great chances I had to have some fun with my students! We all loved it and our students were looking forward to the days of these crazy events!

When I began my tenure as building principal, I had the great opportunity to come on our classroom television monitors and do my best news anchorman imitation with our morning announcements. While nobody was going to be calling me for a national newscast spot anytime soon, this daily routine gave my students and staff an opportunity to see me in a different light and have a few chuckles as well. Each morning I would welcome the students, announce any events going on, share the lunch menu, wish happy birthdays and I ALWAYS closed with two things. I charged the students to "GO LEARN SOMETHING" and then the world famous "Joke of the Day"! The elementary students loved the jokes and the teachers laughed at me more than the punch line!

Again, don't we want the students to look forward to coming to our school? Whatever it takes!

The many faces of having fun with my students!

Suggestions for having FUN with your Students!

☐ Talk with your PTO when they need to raise money for a specific purchase and volunteer to do something crazy as an incentive for the students!

☐ For elementary leaders, pick days to go outside for recess with the students and jump in a dodge ball game, touch football and simply swing on the swings with them.

☐ Get your "groove on" at one of the school dances.

☐ Show your musical talent and sign up for the students' talent show!

☐ Coax a group of your fellow administrators and perform your favorite 80s hit during the school's lip sync contest!

<u>Staff</u> (FUN)

As you begin to grow with your staff, you will see that you all become a family away from your family. As with your own family enjoyment comes during those fun moments in your life! You begin to look forward to having more of those to create special long-lasting memories. Fun is a key component we need to have in the business of education. As you lead your building look for opportunities to laugh with your staff members. Have fun with them. Make memories like you do with your own family! Can you think of a fun time period that you and your family had over your years? Was it a picnic, birthday gathering, trip to a Theme Park? These are times that you remember for the rest of your life and make you long for the day when you can revisit that feeling.

My parents, Jack and Judy Birmingham, made a concerted effort to have fun with our family and yes, making time and saving dollars to vacation in Disney World was one of the memories that my folks wanted to share the fun and enjoyment with us. Maybe not so much the 22-hour ride in the Ford Country Squire as I mentioned earlier, as long before the IPHONE and "in-car" VCRS, my sisters and I had to learn "the license plate game", "car bingo" or how to basically annoy each other. Oh yeah, in the mid-70s most cars did not have air conditioning either, so no real conversations occurred when all of our window were "rolled" down to help combat the 120-degree temperature in the vehicle through Florida. However, when you combine the strange smells of black coffee, cheese puffs and feet, we quickly realized how grateful we were to have those windows all the way down! Remember the saying of "getting there is half the fun"? Half the fun was drastically overestimated. But once we arrived…it was all worth it! The memories are as vivid today as they were back then.

Can you think of any specific time that the fun was overflowing in your building and you sensed that your staff felt glad to be there? I can recall many instances where it was simply a great time to be hanging with my staff. From carry-ins, surprise birthday celebrations to "Jack's Grillfest", I tried to always give the staff an opportunity to put the pressures of their day behind them and simply relax and laugh. We have all heard that "laughter is the best medicine" and many times as a leader we need to fill those prescriptions!

<u>**Suggestions for having FUN with your Staff**</u>

☐ Arrange to bring in a breakfast treat to sit and enjoy with your staff one morning. Talk about anything EXCEPT school.

☐ Help orchestrate an evening out event. Go to a play, sporting event or simply pick a local establishment to get together for a social gathering.

☐ Set up a picnic outside your school building on a beautiful day so that your staff members can skip the teacher's lounge and eat outside. Make sure to be the grill master for the hot dogs and hamburgers!

Parents (FUN)

While the parents/guardians are a little more challenging to find time to have fun with, one thing that you must show them is that you enjoy being in your role as the leader of their students' building. They will appreciate the fact that it looks like a fun place to be because of your leadership. You will want your students to tell stories of how fun school was today. No matter the grade!

Additionally, the fun you show can carry outside your building and off school hours. Make the extra effort to be a part of extracurricular events, league games and concerts. Find an opportunity to show your interests to the parents and students. They eat this up! For example, over the years when I served as the building principal I had the wonderful opportunity to throw out the first pitch at our little league opening day ceremony, play on staff basketball teams during a community fundraiser basketball game and dress up like "The Grinch" during our Christmas Programs. This is one of my favorite things to do. Not only does this show the parents that I enjoy participating as a part of their community, but they get to see me having fun in a different role, still representing the school as their leader.

<u>**Suggestions to have FUN with your parents!**</u>

❏ Volunteer to work in a community cleanup project with some of the parents in your school.

❏ Be a part of a foursome with some of the stakeholders in your district at the Athletic Department golf outing.

❏ Lend a helping hand in the football concession stand with the Band Boosters.

❏ Do a "cameo" appearance at one of the school plays.

When the Ride is CLOSED FOR REPAIR!

Now I truly get it. You may be reading this book saying, "I have a hard time having fun with some of my students, staff and even parents. Have you seen how they are?" Well actually, I have. Every building has those negative influences that simply find no enjoyment...in having fun! So how do you promote having fun in that environment? By simply focusing on two important things. Number one, don't let them steal your joy. You continue to smile and find those who seek the fun that you are trying to spread throughout. Truthfully, the old adage of "killing them with kindness" is vitally important here! It is their choice to be miserable in a building experiencing fun, not yours. In a theme park, I don't see too many people who pay for their ticket, walk ten steps into the park and then say, "look at all of these people laughing and having a blast, this isn't for me"! In fact, when you think of a true theme park, look at all of the opportunities a patron has to find "fun".

For the smallest to the tallest, youngest to the oldest, there is something that the park has to offer for each of them. I can recall tons of options we had at our fingertips at these amusement parks that didn't revolve around the main attraction rides. Arcades, water parks, musicals, train rides and museums are now all commonplace at our nation's most sought after parks. Let's not forget about those "midway games" that entice us to spend hundreds of dollars to "win" a seven-foot minion by tossing a softball into an apple basket or making three free throws in a basketball hoop that is 3 inches smaller than regulation!

Nonetheless, these are a few of the many ways that theme parks strive to create opportunities for their patrons to have fun. As a building leader, make a point to do a fun audit with your groups as well. What is fun to you might not be fun to them and you might have to work at it. This can be as simple as a quick survey at the start of the school year. Ask what your staff like to do for fun? Travel? Read? Exercise? By simply asking what they enjoy, shows that you care about their experiences here in your school.

Are We There Yet???

How do you know when you have arrived at your THEME PARK?

Are we there yet? Are we there yet? Are we there yet? How about now? No parent that has ever taken their children on a vacation to a theme park, is immune to hearing this question...at least once for every state they pass through and then add another for every billboard strewn along the interstate advertising the wonderful world that awaits them!

Of course, most of these don't always tell how far away they are. Just that they are "getting closer"! These signs appear more often as you get closer to the park, telling you that indeed you are almost there until you see a giant "Welcome" sign and a parking lot. But how about your school's climate? How do you know when you have moved from a carnival to a theme park climate? You don't have any billboards to put up that say, "WE RESPECT ALL" or "WE TRUST PEOPLE…TRUST US!" or "COME SEE HOW FUN WE ARE!"

There will be some things to look for that are indicators of your building beginning to morph into a theme park climate. Look for these signs in particular.

First, are you noticing that parent complaints and requests for particular teachers are declining? This is a sure sign that your stakeholders/parents are comfortable with the overall climate of the building and trust the staff members at all grades and subject levels. While you may not have 100% satisfaction initially, once you begin to develop your climate, you will start to see a noticeable decline in those requests from parents to avoid certain teachers.

Secondly, have you seen that your teachers' and students' attendance rate is on the upswing? Let's face it. Theme Parks are crowded most of the time. Why is it? BECAUSE IT IS A GREAT PLACE TO BE! The same can be said about your school. If you set out to create a climate built on trust, respect and fun you will notice that your teachers and students love being there. They will not find reasons to miss school! When your teachers are there, learning occurs. That is the main point!

Finally, are your students, staff and stakeholders initiating new strategies to strengthen the trust, respect and fun? Much like the child that wants to rush to the next ride without holding your hand, those groups of people we are trying to reach will soon understand how the trust, respect and fun concepts work and will begin creating strategies on their own. With our without you! They love what was created and will look to continue the climate that they enjoy being a part of.

This process won't be easy. It will take some time for you to develop a climate that can serve as a jumping off point for a sustained culture. Typically, three years is the average length of how long this can take. Be patient. Don't quit! In the end your students will be better for your efforts.

Remember what the goal is. To be a theme park NOT a carnival. Carnivals get set up within a week and torn day in a day. Your "theme park" will take time, but much like true theme parks, once it has a strong foundation it will remain for years!

In Closing

In closing, it is worth mentioning that in all of these three areas, YOU will need to make the initiative in developing the connections. YOU can't simply sit back and let trust, respect and fun happen. Because it won't. This is YOUR building. If YOU want to create a climate that will turn into something wonderful, you need to drive it. I can only guess that the fact that you have read this book, indicates that a warm, welcoming climate is something you want your school to have. We all do. It will take some work, but it is not impossible. I will tell you that as you embark on this process, you will experience healthy relationships, rewarding results and the confidence in knowing that you will have students, staff and parents all clamoring to be a part of this special "theme park" that you have created. I wish you luck and look forward to the stories of your wonderful transformation. Possibly on those silent 8mm films?

Author Jack Birmingham is an educator who truly believes in relational leadership, Jack Birmingham began his teaching career in 1988 and then transitioned into an administrative career in 2001. He has teaching and principal experience with all grade levels within 6 different school corporations in Indiana and currently serves as Assistant Superintendent for Union Township School Corporation in Valparaiso, Indiana. Additionally, he has serves as a state mentor to Indiana Principals and presents on the topic of school climate at state workshops and conferences frequently.

Jack has been married to his wife Doreen since 1991 and they have four wonderful children, Tyler, Maranda, Gracie and Serena